TreeTops

14

Comprehension

PUPILS' BOOK

5

Catherine Baker
and Charlotte Raby

OXFORD
UNIVERSITY PRESS

OXFORD
UNIVERSITY PRESS

Great Clarendon Street, Oxford OX2 6DP

Oxford University Press is a department of the University of Oxford.
It furthers the University's objective of excellence in research, scholarship, and education by publishing worldwide in

Oxford New York
Auckland Cape Town Dar es Salaam Hong Kong Karachi
Kuala Lumpur Madrid Melbourne Mexico City Nairobi
New Delhi Shanghai Taipei Toronto

With offices in
Argentina Austria Brazil Chile Czech Republic France Greece
Guatemala Hungary Italy Japan Poland Portugal Singapore
South Korea Switzerland Thailand Turkey Ukraine Vietnam

Extracts and activities compiled by Catherine Baker

British Library Cataloguing in Publication Data

Data available

ISBN: 978-0-19-846747-2

7 9 10 8 6

Printed in China by Imago

Acknowledgements

The copyright for each extract is held by the Author, unless otherwise stated. Extracts (in order of appearance): *Cool Clive and the Little Pest* by Michaela Morgan, TreeTops Fiction Stage 12 More Stories A; *Spooky!* by Michaela Morgan, adapted by David Calcutt, TreeTops Playscripts Stage 13; *Fayim's Incredible Journey* by Tessa Krailing, TreeTops True Stories Stage 12, © Brooke Hospital for Animals, Charity No: 1085760; 'Rising Sea Levels' from *Save Our Coasts!* by Sarah Fleming, TreeTops Non-Fiction Stage 13; 'The River Cinquains' by Nigel Cox from *Poetry 2* by John Foster (Macmillan Publishers, 1986); *Snooty Prune* by Pippa Goodhart, TreeTops Fiction Stage 12 More Stories A; *Race Against Time* by Paul May, TreeTops True Stories Stage 14; 'Stop Global Warming!' from *Changing State* by David Glover, Oxford Connections; *The Quest for the Golden See-Saw* by Karen Wallace, TreeTops Fiction Stage 13 More Stories B; 'A Tomcat Is' by J Patrick Lewis from *The Moonlit Stream and Other Poems*, Oxford Literacy Web; 'A Foxy Move' from *Animals and Us* by Claire Llewellyn, TreeTops Non-Fiction Stage 14; *The Terrible Power of House Rabbit* by Susan Gates, TreeTops Fiction Stage 14 More Stories A; *Grace the Pirate* by James Riordan, TreeTops Fiction Stage 14; 'Apollo 13' from *Changing State* by David Glover, Oxford Connections; *Petey* by Paul Shipton, adapted by David Calcutt, TreeTops Playscripts Stage 14; 'Roman Letters' from *Write Now* by Elaine Canham, TreeTops Non-Fiction Stage 14; *Climbing in the Dark* by Nick Warburton, TreeTops Fiction Stage 14; *Petey* by Paul Shipton, adapted by David Calcutt, TreeTops Playscripts Stage 14; 'All About the Sun' from *The Power of Nature* by Becca Heddle, TreeTops Non-Fiction Stage 14; 'The Way Through the Woods' by Rudyard Kipling from *The Way Through the Woods and Other Poems*, Oxford Literacy Web.

The Publisher would like to thank the following for permission to reproduce photographs: **p16** Corbis/Steve Kaufman; **p24** Corbis/Digital Image 1996; **p26**t Corbis/Bill Gentile; **p26**l Science Library/Martin Bond; **p26**r Corbis/Farrell Grehan; **p44**t NASA; **p44**m Corbis; **p45** Corbis/Bettmann; **p50** Corbis/Patrick Ward; **p51** Heritage Museum/British Museum; **p60** Science Photo Library/ Mehau Kulyk.

Cover photograph by NASA

Illustrations: **pp6, 7** Dee Shulman; **pp9, 10, 11** Stephen Lewis; **pp13, 14** Kim Harley; **p16** Mark Duffin; **pp18, 19** Anna Menzies; **pp21, 22** Peter Kavanah; **p27** Martin Aston; **p29** Judy Brown; **p32** Peet Ellison; **pp36, 37, 38** Martin Remphry; **pp40, 41** Steve Hutton; **p45** David Russell; **pp47, 48, 57, 58** Chris Smedley; **p50** Stefan Chabluk; **pp53, 54, 55** Martin Cottam; **p60** Stefan Chabluk; **pp62, 63** Alan Marks.

Although every effort has been made to contact the owners of copyright material, a few have been impossible to trace. However, if they contact the Publisher, correct acknowledgement will be made in future editions.

Design by PDQ Digital Media Solutions Ltd

Paper used in the production of this book is a natural, recyclable product made from wood grown in sustainable forests. The manufacturing process conforms to the environmental regulations of the country of origin.

Note to teachers

The texts in this book are differentiated for use with pupils of different reading abilities.
easiest text, medium text, most difficult text

Contents

Introduction

How comprehension strategies can help you

Have you ever read something, and then thought to yourself, 'What was that all about?' Or read a page of text and then had to go straight back and read it again because you'd already forgotten it? This probably happens to everyone from time to time – but luckily there's a way to avoid it! If you practise using the four key comprehension strategies below, they will help you to get the most out of everything you read, whether it's fiction, non-fiction, poetry or drama.

Predicting

- You probably already know how to use headings and pictures or diagrams to help you work out what a text will be about. But did you know you can use prediction at any time when you're reading, not just at the start?
- When you've finished reading one paragraph or section, you can predict what the next one will be about – this helps you keep tabs on what's happening throughout the text.
- You can even use prediction to help you work out what the next sentence will be about!
- Sometimes you'll find that your predictions were wrong. If this happens, you can always go back and reread the text (or part of it) to help you understand what's going on. Then you can make a new prediction.

Imagining

- As you read, think about the pictures in your head – pictures of the characters in a story, or pictures of a scene from a play or poem, or pictures from a description in a non-fiction text.
- Building up these pictures in your head can help you to understand the text.
- Don't forget to use all your senses as you read – what would it be like to be there? What would you see, hear, feel, touch, smell …?

- As you read on, you can add to the picture you have of the text – and sometimes you will find that you have to change the picture as you read!
- You can also use drawing, or drama techniques such as role-play and hot-seating, to help you imagine the text.

Questioning & clarifying

- Good readers keep on asking questions in their heads as they read.
- When you are reading fiction, you can ask questions about why the characters feel or behave the way they do. Why do certain things happen in the story? How does one thing lead to another?
- When you are reading non-fiction, asking lots of questions helps you to understand the text and make links between different parts of the text. It also helps you make links with what you already know about the subject.
- In any type of text, you can ask questions about the word choices the author made, or the message they want us to take away as readers.
- Use the 'look-back' strategy to help you answer your questions by looking back in the text for the answers. You can also use what you already know about the subject – or your own imagination – to answer your questions.
- It can help to keep a note of your questions and come back to them later, or talk about them with someone else who has read the text.

Summarising

- Summarising helps you focus on the most important information in the text, or the main things that happen in the story.
- When you read fiction, summarising can help you retell the story, write a book review or a blurb, or give reasons when you recommend a book to a friend.
- When you read non-fiction, summarising can help you work out the main point of the text, and how the different parts of the text work together.
- Summarising can also help you sum up the author's style, their intention in writing the text, the way the text is put together, etc.

COOL CLIVE AND THE LITTLE PEST

Questioning & clarifying

What kind of person is Clive (the narrator of the story)? How do you know?

My little sister, Jade, has been trouble since the day she was born.
I remember the day Mum brought her home from the hospital. I'd been promised a sister who would be fun to play with. I got a red-faced, wrinkled, soggy little bundle.

Everyone adored her…
and everyone ignored me.

All the time she was a baby
I kept an eye on her.
When she lost things…
I found them.

When she made a mess… I helped clean it up.

When she learnt to walk… I caught her.

Yes, I caught her. I taught her… and sometimes I fought her.

And sometimes I felt just a bit fed up.

She has always had annoying habits
– like collecting animals.
If she sees a lonely ladybird,
she brings it home.

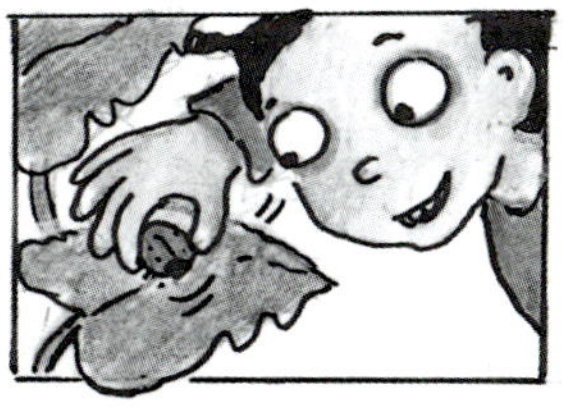

If she sees a wandering worm,
she brings it home.

If she sees a slimy snail,
she brings it home.

Our house is like a zoo sometimes. Especially when Jade's animals escape.

So you see, she really was a little pest when she was a baby but now that she's five she's...

Still, she is my sister and she does have her good points...

...and so
I agreed to keep an eye on her.

Cool Clive and the Little Pest

Partner activities

I can ...

- **use evidence from the text to work out what might happen next**
- **write a story plan to show this**

1. Read the text, and then talk with your partner about what you think will happen when Clive keeps an eye on Jade. Think about what you know about both characters from the text. Decide between you how the story might end.
2. Together, write a story plan that shows what happens next and how the story ends. Then you can write the story, or act it out for your teacher or another pair.

Predicting

Think about what Jade is like, and what Clive is like. What could go wrong when Clive looks after Jade?

Think and write

1. How did Clive feel when Jade was born, and why?
2. What did Clive do for Jade when she was a baby? Name three things.
3. Clive says Jade 'has been trouble since the day she was born'. Do you think this is fair? Why, or why not?
4. What does Jade do nowadays that Clive finds annoying?
5. Why does Clive find this annoying?
6. How do you think the animals feel about being collected by Jade? Explain why you think this.
7. Clive says that Jade 'does have her good points'. Name two of them.
8. Imagine you are Jade. Write three sentences to explain how you feel about Clive.
9. Find a quote from the story where the author uses rhyme. Why do you think the author does this?
10. Do you think the pictures go well with the words in this text? Why or why not?

From *Spooky!*, adapted by David Calcutt from the original book by Michaela Morgan, TreeTops Playscripts Stage 13, pages 41–47.

Spooky!

Questioning & clarifying

What do you think of Miss Jackson's story? Do you think the mill might really be haunted?

Martin, Katie, Alice and their class are on a school trip to an old mill. Some people say that it's haunted – but is that just an old story?

__Katie__ and __Alice__ sit. __Miss Jackson__ sits and tells the story.

Miss Jackson Right, then. Here's the story. Once, long ago, a miller and his wife lived here. The miller was fond of drink, but he was not fond of hard work.

The person who plays __Joe__ enters as the __miller__, drinking from a jug.

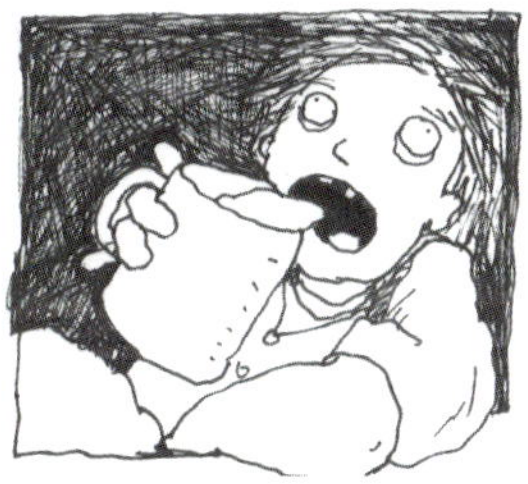

Miller I love my ale! Why should I work? My wife can do all the work and leave me to drink my ale!

He drinks.

Miss Jackson His wife wasn't happy about this, of course. And she made sure the miller knew how unhappy she was.

The person who plays __Marge__ enters as the __miller's wife__.

Wife There's no end to this work! I never stop, morning, noon and night! And what do you do to help? Nothing!

Miller Be quiet with your nagging, woman!

Miss Jackson And so it went on, for years –

Wife All you do is sit and drink your ale!

Miller That's just as it should be!

Miss Jackson And years –

Wife What are you good for? Nothing!

Miller Shut up, woman, and leave me in peace!

Miss Jackson And years!

Wife You're just a lazy, good-for-nothing drunkard! And it's not fair or right!

*The **miller's wife** goes.*

Miller That wife of mine! I'm tired of her nagging. I wish I could find a way to make her shut up.

Miss Jackson And one day that good-for-nothing miller had an idea – an awful, terrible idea!

Miller That's it! I know just what to do!

*The **miller** goes.*

Miss Jackson He came up this room, Room One. It was the place where they used to store the malt. The floor in those days was just loose planks of wood laid down on the beams. He came up here and took one of those planks away. And when his wife brought a sack of malt up here, she put her foot down – on nothing! And she fell down to her death!

*Off stage, the **miller's wife** screams. The **miller** enters.*

Miller That's put an end to her nagging. Now I'll have me a quiet life!

Miss Jackson But he was wrong. From that day on he had no peace, or quiet. Because his wife haunted him.

*The **miller's wife** enters. The **miller** sees her.*

Wife I'll haunt you all your days. I'll never let you rest. You'll have no peace from me!

*The **miller** cries out.*

Miller No! No! No!

He runs off.

Miss Jackson He went mad. He left the mill. It looked as if the mill would go to ruin. But it didn't. Because as soon as he'd gone, the mill started to shine.

Wife Now the place is mine. I'll always keep it tidy and clean. And there'll always be a welcome for whoever comes here.

She goes.

Miss Jackson People say it's the ghost of the miller's wife still looking after the place. She's happy in her work now the miller has gone. But of course, it's just a story. No one really believes in ghosts –

***Martin** enters.*

Martin All right! Who's the joker?

Miss Jackson Martin – !

Martin Who's been in my room and tidied all the stuff away?

Miss Jackson What's that?

Martin I went to tidy my room, like you said, and somebody had already done it!

Spooky!

Partner activities

I can ...

- **work out why a character behaves the way she does**
- **take part in a role-play to explore this**

1. Read the text and think about why the miller's wife might have wanted to haunt the mill after her death. Discuss this with your partner.
2. One of you should take on the role of the miller's wife, and the other should ask questions to find out what the miller's wife thinks of her husband and how she feels now that she is a ghost.

Summarising

Use clues from the whole of the text to help you work out what the miller's wife might think and feel.

Think and write

1. Think of three words to describe the miller, and explain why you chose them.
2. Find a quotation from the miller's wife that shows what she thinks of her husband.
3. What idea did the miller have, to make his wife shut up?
4. Did the miller's idea work?
5. Find a quotation that shows whether the narrator (Miss Jackson) is on the miller's side or the wife's side.
6. Why did the miller leave the mill in the end?
7. What happened to the mill when he left, and why?
8. Who do you think tidied Martin's room? Explain why.
9. Why do you think the author chose to have the story acted out by characters in role as the miller and his wife, rather than just letting Miss Jackson tell the story?
10. Do you think the miller's wife was happier when she was alive, or when she was a ghost? Explain your answer.

Fayim's Incredible Journey

Questioning & clarifying

This text is based on a true story. Which bits do you think might be completely true, and which bits might the author have had to make up?

Fayim and his family are forced out of their home because of war. They have to make a terrifying journey across the mountains of Afghanistan to get to safety.

By the time they reached the horse trading post, Fayim was exhausted. Dazed, he stared at the crowds. Everyone seemed to be shouting at the tops of their voices.

Suddenly Baby stopped, rolling his eyes in terror, and refused to budge. Fayim looked round, just in time to see his father and brothers disappear into the crowd.

"Dad! Abdul! Khalid!" he yelled. But it was no use. They couldn't hear him. Fayim put both arms round Baby's neck, too tired to go on. For the first time since he left home, he began to cry. This was a terrible place. He wished they had never come.

"Hey, kid! What's the matter?"

Fayim looked up to see a boy not much older than himself. He wiped away his tears on the back of his sleeve. "I – I've lost my family," he said. "And my donkey's sick. He has sore feet."

"You'd better take him over there."

The boy jerked his head towards a small crowd gathered round a parked van. "The vet comes specially to cure sick animals. He'll soon put your donkey right."

"Thanks!" Fayim pulled Baby towards the van.

The vet was a tall man in a white coat. He picked up Baby's sore feet and looked at them closely. Then he gave Fayim a small pot of ointment and showed him how to put it on.

"Fayim! What do you think you're doing?"

Fayim jumped at the sound of his father's angry voice. "Oh, Dad – this man's an animal doctor. He's given me some stuff to put on Baby's feet."

"Are you mad? You know we can't afford to pay for medicines." His father looked very worried. "Give it back to him. Tell him you don't want it."

"It's free," said a man in a grey turban. "You don't have to pay."

"Free?" His father looked stunned. "But how – ?"

"This is an animal clinic," the man explained. "The vet comes every day to treat the horses."

His father shook his head wonderingly.

"Perhaps he would treat ours, too? Some of them are very weak."

Fayim caught his sleeve. "Dad, you're not angry with me, are you?"

His father shook his head. "No, son. I'm not angry. You've looked after Baby well. I'm proud of you."

"But are you going to sell him?" Fayim asked, anxiously.

"Sell him? Of course not. Baby is our future. He'll be almost all we have to start again, once we've sold the horses." His father smiled. "Khalid has gone to the camp to find your mother and sisters. Soon we shall all be together again."

Fayim felt so happy he gave Baby a hug. "We did it!" he whispered in the little donkey's ear. "We're only young but we walked over the mountains. And now we're going to make a new start, Baby. You and me!"

Fayim's Incredible Journey

Partner activities

I can ...

- find clues in the text that tell me how the main character's feelings change
- draw a diagram to represent this

1. With your partner, make notes on how Fayim's feelings change at different points in the text. You should be able to find at least six different feelings.
2. Together, make a diagram to show all the different feelings Fayim goes through. One way of doing this is to draw a Feelings Graph, with Fayim's feelings (from saddest to happiest) on the vertical axis, and the events in the story on the horizontal axis. You can then mark how Fayim was feeling at each event in the story, and draw a line to join the feelings.

Imagining

Imagine you are Fayim – how would you be feeling?

Think and write

1. Who is Baby?
2. How does Fayim feel when they get to the horse trading post, and why?
3. Why do you think Fayim is crying when the boy talks to him?
4. Why do you think Fayim's dad sounds angry when he finds him?
5. What does the vet do to help Fayim?
6. What surprises Fayim's dad about the vet?
7. Why isn't Fayim's dad cross with him?
8. How does Fayim feel about Baby? Find at least two pieces of evidence for this.
9. Why does Fayim's dad say 'Baby is our future'?
10. Whose point of view is this story told from? How do you know?

Summarising

When you've read this text, try to sum up in just one sentence what it is mostly about.

Rising sea levels

Sea levels on Earth are linked with temperature. The Earth's temperature changes all the time. It changes in a yearly cycle from winter to summer, but it also has a cycle of colder and hotter periods that last hundreds of thousands of years. For example, there has been an Ice Age about once every 100,000 years.

When the Earth gets cold, the sea level drops. This is because water on land freezes and stops flowing into the sea.

When the Earth gets hotter, the sea level rises because the sea's volume increases. This can happen in two ways:

- the sea gets warmer so the water expands. The same amount of water takes up more space as it heats up
- ice on land melts and extra water flows into the sea. Water melts that was frozen and 'trapped' as ice on land in glaciers (flowing ice rivers) and in ice sheets (huge areas of ice).

If all the glaciers melted, the sea level would rise by about 0.3 metres.

This glacier flows down to the coast of Argentina from the Patagonian ice sheet in South America.

The biggest ice sheets are on the Antarctic (which is a land continent) and Greenland. If they melted completely, the sea level on Earth would rise by 80 metres.

Rising sea levels

Partner activities

I can ...

- read a text and make notes to help me understand it
- explain what the text is saying to my partner

1. When you have read the text, find the part that explains how sea levels rise when Earth gets hotter. Reread this part and make notes to help you remember the two ways in which sea levels can rise.
2. Using your notes (but not looking at the text) explain to your partner how sea levels rise.
3. With your partner, talk about what you think the effects of rising sea levels might be.

Questioning & clarifying

If you're not sure what the text is telling you, go back and reread the text to clarify it.

Think and write

1. What are the two cycles of temperature change mentioned in the text?
2. How often do Ice Ages occur?
3. What effect does it have on sea levels when the Earth becomes cold?
4. Explain how the sea level could go up when the Earth gets hotter, even if there is no extra water.
5. What happens to sea levels when ice on land melts?
6. What is the difference between a glacier and an ice sheet?
7. If you were worried about rising sea levels, would you be more concerned about glaciers melting, or about ice sheets melting? Why?
8. Name one place on Earth where there are glaciers, according to the text.
9. Name one ice sheet other than those on the Antarctic and Greenland.
10. How well do you think this text explains how sea levels rise? Think of one thing you could add to improve it.

'The River Cinquains' by Nigel Cox from Oxford Literacy Web, *The Moonlit Stream and other poems*, pages 14–15.

Summarising

When you have read this sequence of poems, try to sum up in one or two sentences what they are about.

The River Cinquains

Dawn
Daybreak:
Between grey rocks,
Silently it wells up
With the force of blood from a wound:
Water.

Morning
Moorland:
Purple heather.
Early sun lights the stream:
Rushing, chattering, swift with fish,
Sparkling.

Afternoon
Townscape:
Water reflects
Grey brickwork, dull windows.
Fishermen stare. The river moves
Slowly.

Evening
Salt-marsh:
Under lead skies
The water slides away.
From the damp banks of sand a few
Birds call.

Night
Moon shines
On open sea:
The swell gleams with silver
And on a distant shore the first
Waves break.

Nigel Cox

The River Cinquains

Partner activities

I can …

- **read a sequence of poems and decide which is my favourite and why**
- **draw a picture to illustrate the poem so my partner can guess which it is**

1. Read the cinquains, and decide which you like best. Write notes to explain why you chose it – think about the meaning, the words, the way it sounds, etc.
2. Draw a picture to illustrate your favourite cinquain. Then swap with your partner – can you tell which poem they were illustrating?
3. Discuss with your partner why you chose your cinquain. Do you agree with each other's choices?

Imagining

Read the cinquains aloud, and think about the pictures you see in your head as you hear the words.

Think and write

1. Does this sequence of cinquains describe one river or lots of different rivers? Explain your answer.
2. In which cinquain is the river smallest?
3. What is happening in the last cinquain, 'Night'?
4. In 'Dawn', what does the poet compare the water of the river to?
5. Do you think this is an effective comparison? Explain why, or why not.
6. Which cinquain shows the river moving quickly?
7. What mood do you think the poet is trying to capture in 'Afternoon'? Find two quotes that help to express this mood.
8. In 'Evening', do you think the sky is dark or bright? Which word gives you a clue about this?
9. In 'Night', what does the phrase 'The swell gleams with silver' mean?
10. Which cinquain do you think is the most effective? Explain why.

From *Snooty Prune* by Pippa Goodhart,
TreeTops Stage 12 More Stories A, pages 4–13.

Snooty Prune

Summarising

As you read, think about how you would feel if you were Prunella.

Prunella was very tall. She was the tallest in her class. She had to look down when she talked to the other children. She couldn't help it.

But the other children didn't like it.

'You're snooty!' said a girl called Beth. 'A snooty prune!' Everyone laughed. So Beth said it again.

Then they all said it. For days and weeks they went on. They used it as her name all the time.

Prunella hated it. And she hated the children at school for using it. Most of all she hated Beth. But she didn't want to hate people. What she really wanted was a friend. Prunella wished very hard for a friend.

One day the doorbell rang. It was Mrs Farey at the door. Mrs Farey lived over the road. She was interesting. She wore strange clothes and kept ducks and cats. Prunella liked her.

Finger by finger, Mrs Farey opened out her hand to show a tiny parcel. 'It's very little,' she said. 'But I hope that it will bring you your biggest wish!'

'Thank you!' said Prunella.

'That's all right, my dear,' said Mrs Farey. 'Happy day!'

Prunella looked at the tiny parcel. It was very thin and wrapped in paper the colour of cats' eyes.

She pulled the parcel gently open. Inside was a tiny red book of stamps.

'What a strange present!' said her mother. But Prunella knew that the stamps were a wonderful present. Those tiny bits of sticky paper would let you send messages to anyone in the world. With a stamp you could write to the Prime Minister or the Queen. You could send off for things.

Or you could send a sneaky letter to school to tell them that Beth Hall was a bully. But Prunella didn't want to sneak on Beth.

What she really wanted to do was to write to a friend. A friend would write back. If only she had a friend.

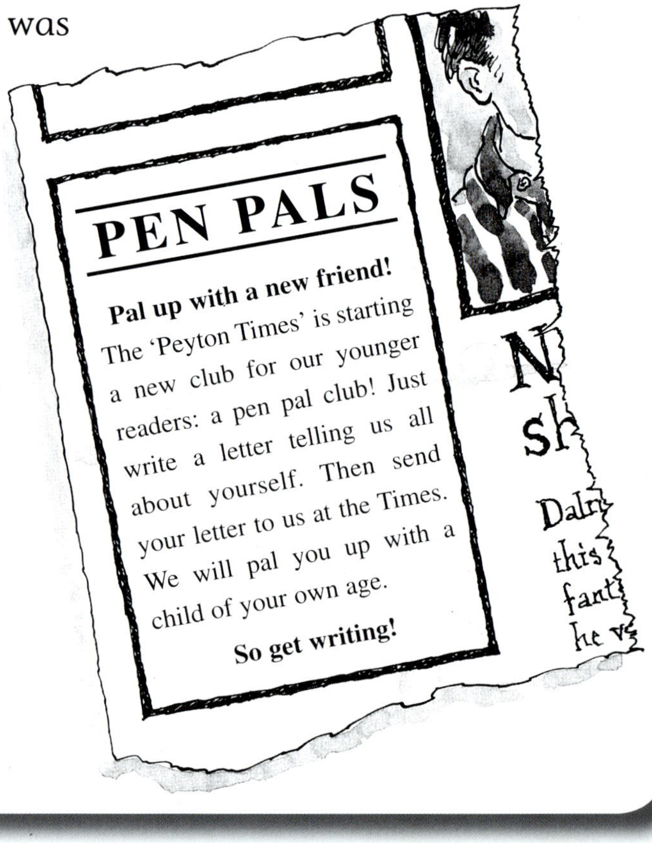

PEN PALS

Pal up with a new friend!

The 'Peyton Times' is starting a new club for our younger readers: a pen pal club! Just write a letter telling us all about yourself. Then send your letter to us at the Times. We will pal you up with a child of your own age.

So get writing!

Prunella stood up and something fell to the floor.

It was a small, folded bit of newspaper. It had been put into the parcel with the stamps.

Prunella opened it out and read.

I will, thought Prunella. I'll make a pen pal friend!

Oh, thank you, Mrs Farey!

Snooty Prune

Partner activities

I can ...

- work out what two characters in a text are like
- use role-play to explore the relationship between the characters

1. Read the text, and then talk with your partner about Prunella and Beth. What are they like? What can you find out about them from the text? What would you think of them if you met them?
2. Role-play being Prunella and Beth. Beth should explain why she behaves as she does, and Prunella should explain how she feels.

Questioning & clarifying

Look for clues about the characters in what they say and do, and in what the text says about them.

Think and write

1. What is it that the other children don't like about Prunella?
2. What do they do to let her know they don't like her?
3. Do you think Prunella did anything to deserve being treated like this?
4. What kind of person is Mrs Farey?
5. Why do you think the author chose the name Mrs Farey for this character?
6. What is in the present that Mrs Farey gives Prunella?
7. How does Prunella feel about Mrs Farey's present, and why?
8. What are the four things that Prunella thinks you could do with Mrs Farey's present?
9. What does Prunella decide to do with the present in the end?
10. What do you think will happen next in this story, and how will it end? Write at least three sentences to explain what you think will happen.

Race Against Time

Predicting

Take a quick look at the text – what kind of text do you think it is?

The spacecraft Apollo 13 is on its way to the Moon.

"13, this is Houston," said Mission Control.

"Go ahead, Houston," Jim replied.

"We'd like you to check your thrusters. And then we'd like you to stir your oxygen tanks."

"*OK*," said Jim. "*Stand by*."

Inside Odyssey's service module, two tanks held the oxygen that kept the crew alive. The astronauts breathed the oxygen, and the oxygen did other jobs too. It mixed with hydrogen to make water, and even helped to make electricity to power the spacecraft. The oxygen was so cold that it was nearly solid, and sometimes it had to be stirred to keep it moving. Jack reached up and flicked a switch.

Ninety seconds went by. The astronauts were busy with their jobs. Fred Haise was floating through the tunnel from Aquarius. Suddenly there was a deep thud. The spacecraft shuddered. The walls moved.

Jim looked at Fred. Was this another joke? Then he saw Fred's eyes. There was no joke. Fred was terrified. "*It wasn't me*," he said.

Warning lights flashed on above their heads. An alarm sounded in Jim's ear. Jack stared at the instruments. He couldn't believe what he saw. Half of their power had gone. "*Hey!*" Jack shouted. "*We've got a problem here.*"

The radio crackled. "*This is Houston. Say again, please.*"

"*Houston, we've had a problem*," Jim replied.

Jim Lovell sounded calm, but all the astronauts were thinking the same terrible thought. A meteor must have hit them. And if a meteor had hit them, in seconds they might all be dead.

Race Against Time

Partner activities

I can ...

- **sum up the main things that happen in the text**
- **make a storyboard or cartoon sequence to show what happens**

1. Read the text, and then retell the story of the text in your own words – what happens, and in what order? Make notes to remind you.
2. Together, draw and write a storyboard or cartoon with about three separate pictures, to show the main events in the text and the order in which they happened. Use speech bubbles and captions as well as pictures.

Summarising

Keep thinking about which are the most important things that happen. Which details can you leave out, and which do you need to keep?

Think and write

1. The spacecraft Apollo 13 had two separate parts. What were their names?
2. Why did Houston contact the astronauts?
3. What were the first names of the three astronauts?
4. Why was the store of oxygen so important to the astronauts? Find three reasons.
5. Why did Mission Control ask the astronauts to stir their oxygen tanks?
6. Why did Jim look at Fred when he heard the thud?
7. What was the problem that the astronauts reported to Mission Control?
8. What did the astronauts think had caused the problem?
9. This text is based on a true story, and the words in italic are words that the astronauts actually spoke. Why do you think the author put these words in italic?
10. How would you have been feeling at the end of the text if you were one of the astronauts?

From Oxford Connections: *Changing State*
by David Glover, pages 44–45.

Summarising

When you have read the text, work out which of the two points of view in the text you agree with most.

Stop global warming!

Global warming will cause more of this:

Flooded homes in India

And this:

Drought and famine in Africa

FACT: The world is getting warmer

- Global warming is caused by human activity
- If we do not act now lives will be lost and communities destroyed

You must act to prevent global warming.

What's the cause?

The greenhouse effect causes global warming. Carbon dioxide and other greenhouse gases trap the Sun's heat in the atmosphere. Greenhouse gases released by burning coal, oil and gas in power stations and vehicles are increasing the global greenhouse effect. The more energy we use, the more greenhouse gases we release.

Burning petrol produces carbon dioxide – cut do on driving!

What's the evidence?

The graph (above right) shows that the Earth's average temperature is rising. Research shows that the risin temperatures are linked to increasir human energy consumption.

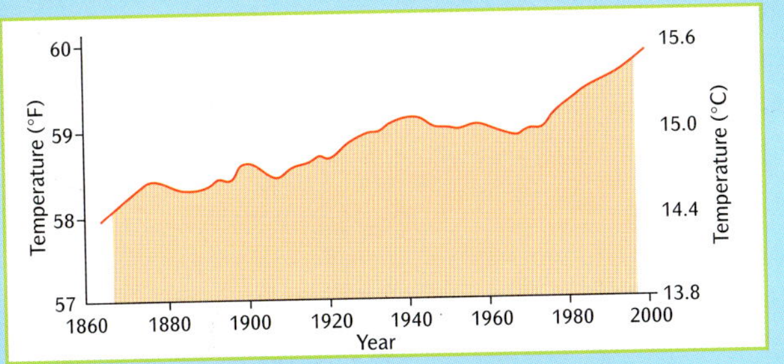

Graph showing how the mean (average) temperature is rising

What are the consequences?

If global warming continues at its present rate droughts and crop failures will become more and more frequent in Africa. Deserts will spread. Millions will starve. Enormous quantities of ice will melt at the poles. Sea levels will rise. Coastal communities around the world will be devastated by floods.

What can you do?

- Conserve energy. Do not leave lights burning or travel by car when you can walk or cycle.
- Use energy efficiently. Make sure your school and home are well insulated. Don't fill the kettle to the brim to make one cup of coffee.
- Find out about alternative energy sources. Solar panels and wind generators do not produce greenhouse gases.
- Ask local politicians to explain what they are doing about global warming. How are they making it easier for local people to conserve energy?

Act now!

Tomorrow it will be too late!

I disagree!

- I'm only one person. Anything I do can't make a difference to global warming.
- It's not what we do in Europe that causes the problem. Americans use far more energy than us.
- In the future people in developing countries will want to use as much energy as Americans and Europeans. What right have we to say they shouldn't?

Stop Global Warming!

Partner activities

I can ...

- work out the writer's point of view from clues
- identify some facts and some opinions in the text

1. Read the main part of the text (not the speech bubble headed 'I disagree!'). Find some quotes to show what the writer thinks and feels about global warming, and discuss this with your partner.
2. Reread the whole text together, and make a list of facts and opinions. Is it always clear which is which? Talk about this with your partner.

Questioning & clarifying

To help you sort out facts and opinions, ask, 'Can the writer prove this? Would most sensible people agree?' If the answer is yes, it is more likely to be a fact. If the answer is no, it is likely to be an opinion.

Think and write

1. How do greenhouse gases contribute to global warming?
2. Why does the author think we should drive less?
3. Name three things the text says will happen as a result of global warming.
4. Why might it be a bad idea to fill the kettle to the brim for just one cup of coffee?
5. Name two other things that the text says you could do to help stop global warming.
6. Name one source of energy that does not contribute to global warming, according to the text.
7. Why do you think the author ends with the words 'Tomorrow it will be too late!'?
8. Why did the author include the line graph? What can we learn from it?
9. Why do you think the author included the section headed 'I disagree!'?
10. Which of the two points of view in this text do you think is more convincing, and why?

From *The Quest for the Golden See-Saw* by Karen Wallace, TreeTops Fiction Stage 13 More Stories B, pages 3–13.

Questioning & clarifying

While you are reading this text, think about how it is similar to a traditional fairy tale, and how it is different.

The Quest for the Golden See-Saw

Grizzle poured out a cup of tea. Then he lifted up a corner of the royal sheet.

A long, whiskery face, like an old parsnip, looked up at him.

'Ah, Grizzle, it's you,' gasped King Codger. 'For a moment …' His head fell back on the pillows.

Poor King Codger. It was always the same bad dream.

His daughter, Wolverina, was chasing him. She was yelling at the top of her voice.

'It's mine! It's mine! Give it! Or else!'

King Codger pulled the bedclothes over his head.

'It's your own fault, Sire,' said Grizzle, who knew all about the king's bad dreams. He stirred ten spoonfuls of sugar into the royal tea mug. 'You should never have told the princesses you were going to retire to the seaside.'

'But I thought Wolverina would be happy to share the kingdom with her sister,' moaned King Codger.

Grizzle made a rude noise. 'Since when has the Lady Wolverina shared anything?'

King Codger closed his eyes. His daughters floated in front of him.

The oldest was called Goldie-Ox. She was just like his dear departed wife: blonde as a haystack, friendly as a kitten, and wide as a drawbridge.

The king frowned. Perhaps she was a bit too friendly. The last time she had hugged him, she nearly cracked his ribs.

And then there was his other daughter, Wolverina. She wasn't like anyone in the family. In fact, Wolverina wasn't like anyone he had ever met – including trolls, goblins and ogres.

Wolverina was bony as a vulture. And as for her nature – the king shuddered. She was just like a wolverine: cunning, bad-tempered, and she had a nasty bite if she didn't get her own way.

King Codger sighed. If only his dear, departed wife hadn't gone dragon-hunting, and taken an umbrella instead of a sword by mistake. 'She'd know what to do,' he muttered to himself, 'if she was still here.'

'I beg your pardon, Sire,' said Grizzle. He laid out a matching tunic and cloak in blue satin with fake leopardskin trim. Despite his troubles, King Codger was always a snappy dresser.

'My wife, Queen Hundridwate, did make me promise to share my kingdom equally,' replied the king. 'They were her last words.' He blushed. 'Apart from the ones addressed to the person who put the umbrella stand in the wrong place.'

'And who could forget them?' thought Grizzle to himself. Even Spangle, the court magician, had never heard anything like it.

And he knew countless oaths uttered by badly-behaved witches.

At that moment, a flash of inspiration hit Grizzle and he almost dropped the crown he was polishing.

'Call for Spangle!' cried Grizzle, trying not to sound too pleased with himself. 'It's about time he stopped fooling around with frogs and princesses.'

'Grizzle, you're a genius!'

King Codger leapt out of bed and jumped about the room as if he had ants in his pants. 'Call for the Ladies Goldie-Ox and Wolverina! We shall settle the future of the kingdom once and for all!'

The Quest for the Golden See-Saw

Partner activities

I can ...

- think about how two characters in a text are similar or different
- draw a diagram or write two paragraphs comparing the two characters

1. What kind of person is King Codger, and what kind of person is Grizzle? With your partner make notes about each of them. Think about which is cleverer, which is more powerful, which is braver, etc.
2. Together, draw a diagram or write two paragraphs to explain what each character is like and how they are similar or different.

Imagining

Think about what the characters look like and how they behave, as well as what they say.

Think and write

1. Where is King Codger at the start of the text?
2. Who is Grizzle?
3. What does the king's bad dream tell us about Wolverina?
4. What do you think Wolverina is talking about when she says, '"It's mine! It's mine! Give it! Or else!"' in the king's dream?
5. How are Wolverina and Goldie-Ox different in appearance?
6. How are they different in personality?
7. What happened to King Codger's wife, Queen Hundridwate?
8. Who is Spangle?
9. Why do you think Grizzle thinks it is a good idea to call for Spangle?
10. The author has chosen the names for the characters carefully: King Codger, Wolverina and Goldie-Ox. For each name, explain why you think the author chose it and what it tells us about the character.

Questioning & clarifying

What do you think the poet thinks of cats? What evidence can you find for this in the poem?

A Tomcat Is

Nightwatchman of corners
Caretaker of naps
Leg-wrestler of pillows
Depresser of laps

A master at whining
And dining on mouse
Afraid of the shadows
That hide in the house

The bird-watching bandit
On needle-point claws
The chief of detectives
On marshmallow paws

A crafty yarn-spinner
A stringer high-strung
A buttermilk moustache
A sandpaper tongue

The dude in the alley
The duke on the couch
Affectionate fellow
Occasional grouch

J Patrick Lewis

A Tomcat Is

Partner activities

I can ...

- find two powerful images in a poem and explain why I think they are powerful
- draw a picture inspired by one of these images

1. Read the text. You and your partner could take turns to read verses out loud.
2. Read the poem carefully to yourself again. Find two images from the poem that you think are effective, and explain to your partner why you think they work well.
3. Choose one of these images and draw a picture to illustrate it. Can your partner work out which image you have chosen?

Imagining

The author doesn't waste any words when he describes the cat. Read each phrase slowly, and think about the pictures you can see in your head.

Think and write

1. Is the cat in the poem brave? Which words in the poem give you a clue about this?
2. What do you think the poet means when he calls the cat 'Depresser of laps'?
3. What can you work out about the cat's attitude to birds from the poem?
4. What does the cat like to drink?
5. Why do you think the poet describes the cat as 'The chief of detectives/On marshmallow paws'?
6. Is the cat friendly? Quote the lines which tell you about this.
7. In what way do you think the cat's tongue might be like sandpaper?
8. Does the poem keep to the same rhythm throughout, or vary in rhythm?
9. What do you think the author means when he calls the cat 'The dude in the alley/The duke on the couch'?
10. Do you think the illustration goes well with this poem? Why, or why not?

From *Animals and Us* by Claire Llewellyn,
TreeTops Non-Fiction Stage 14, pages 26–27

Before you read this text, quickly think about what you already know about foxes. Then read it – does it make you change your mind about foxes in any way?

A foxy move

The fox has had a difficult relationship with people. For centuries it has been shot by farmers protecting their chickens, and hunted for sport and its fur. The fox has moved from the country to cities and towns, and its luck is beginning to change.

Urban benefits

Foxes are clever animals. They have learned that cities make excellent homes. There are plenty of safe, sheltered spots – garages, sheds and railway sidings – where foxes can live and raise their young. Best of all there are thousands of people who provide a year-round supply of food.

What do they eat?

Insects, birds, berries and mice – **rural** foxes eat many kinds of food. Do urban foxes eat the same kind of diet? How much do they scavenge from bins? 600 dead urban foxes had their stomach contents examined to see exactly what they ate. This showed that city pickings were a big part of a fox's diet.

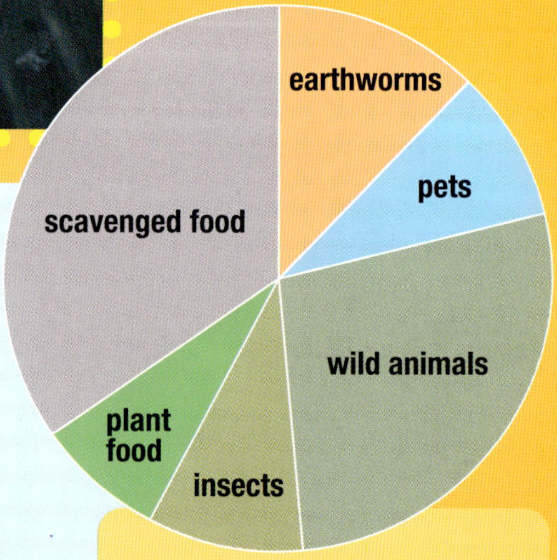

About one third of the food found in foxes' stomachs was made up of city pickings.

A Foxy Move

Partner activities

I can ...

- work out how I feel about foxes based on evidence from the text
- explain my feelings to my partner

1. Read the text. Then decide whether or not you think foxes are a pest in towns. Use evidence from the text and your own ideas. Make notes to remind you.
2. Explain to your partner why you feel like this about foxes. Compare views with your partner. Have you come to the same conclusion, or do you have different ideas? Sum up your views for your teacher or another pair.

Questioning & clarifying

Keep asking yourself questions as you read the text. For example, what damage might foxes do in cities, and what good might they do?

Think and write

1. Why has the fox had 'a difficult relationship with people'?
2. Why do you think the author says that the fox's luck is beginning to change?
3. What is good about cities from a fox's point of view? Find two things.
4. Name two things that a rural fox might eat.
5. Name one way in which an urban fox's diet is different from a rural fox's diet.
6. Why do you think this difference exists?
7. How did scientists find out the information about what urban foxes eat?
8. Do foxes eat only meat, only plant-based food, or a mixture?
9. What do you think is the most surprising thing that urban foxes eat? Explain why you find it surprising.
10. Why do you think the author chose to show the information about the urban foxes' diet as a pie chart?

The Terrible Power of House Rabbit

Questioning & clarifying

As you read, think about what we know about House Rabbit. Do you think Ben is right to be worried about him?

I couldn't stand it any more. I had to tell someone about House Rabbit and how he'd turned my whole family into tidiness freaks.

I sit next to Melissa at school. She's been my best friend since toddler group. So I tried to explain it to her.

'I liked my house messy,' I told her. 'I hate it now! It's not friendly! It smells of disinfectant!'

'And did you say,' Melissa asked, 'that House Rabbit tidies things away?'

'That's right! He's a neatness fanatic! He spends all day tidying up. And now Mum and Dad and Toby are doing it.

'I've even folded up my pyjamas. Can you believe that? It's as if he's cast an evil spell over us all.'

I thought about House Rabbit, all alone in our house. I thought, *I wonder what he's doing now?*

'Rabbits don't tidy up,' said Melissa.

'House Rabbits do.'

'You're just being silly!'

'I'm not! I'm not! Come to my house, on your way home from school. And then you can see for yourself!'

'All right,' Melissa said. 'I will.'

After school, we crept down our garden path. 'Shhh!' I told Melissa. 'We'll surprise him. We'll sneak round the back and look through the windows.'

We peeped through the windows.

'I can't see a rabbit,' said Melissa. 'Are you sure you're not making this up?'

The carpet was as empty as a desert. There wasn't a single brick or book or magazine anywhere.

'He's here all right,' I said, grimly. 'He's probably upstairs.'

We crept into the kitchen.

'Yow!' I nearly crashed on to the kitchen tiles. 'That pesky rabbit! He's been polishing the floor again!'

'Where is he?' asked Melissa.

'Shhh! I'll go and find him.' I crept upstairs and pushed open my bedroom door.

I knew straight away that something was wrong. It didn't feel like my bedroom any more. It didn't even smell like my bedroom. It smelled of disinfectant.

'Oh no!' I yelled. I didn't want to believe it!

But House Rabbit was just coming out from under my bed. He stared at me, as if to say, *That's better! It's nice and tidy now!*

I was outraged! This time he'd gone too far!

'How dare you!' I yelled at him. 'You're not allowed under my bed! Even Mum doesn't go under there!' It's my private place, where I keep all my secrets. All the things I need.

I looked underneath. There was just a big empty space. There was nothing left. Not even a speck of dust.

'Where's my book of *One Thousand Jokes*? Where are my vampire teeth? Where's my favourite bit of blanket?'

Everything had gone. My whole collection of precious, personal things.

'What have you done with my things?' I felt really sick inside.

Then I saw what he'd done. He'd put all my precious things in my wastepaper basket. Just as if they were rubbish!

'Those things aren't rubbish! They're things I need!' I yelled, snatching my bit of blanket out.

It was the last straw. You've got to have one little space. Just one little space that nobody tidies up!

I was hopping mad.

'This is war!' I told House Rabbit. 'It's either you or me. This house isn't big enough for the both of us!'

House Rabbit stayed as calm as custard. He never seemed to get ruffled. He stared at me with those raspberry ice-pop eyes. He didn't blink once. I felt myself going dizzy – and I dropped to my knees.

I started crawling about, with my nose just above the carpet!

'Hummm, I spy a biscuit crumb!'

I told Melissa as she came into my bedroom. 'I must tidy my bedroom! I must pick this up immediately!'

I was just about to pick it up when Melissa saved me.

She grabbed my arm. 'Come on!' she said. She dragged me downstairs. She didn't stop until we reached the garden.

'Phew,' she said. 'I see what you mean – about the terrible power of House Rabbit.'

The Terrible Power of House Rabbit

Partner activities

I can ...

- think about a story from the point of view of one of the characters
- take part in a role-play to explore what that character thinks

1. Read the story, and then talk about what you would have thought if you were Melissa. Would you have believed Ben? When might you have changed your mind, and why?
2. One of you should take the role of Melissa. The other person can ask Melissa what she thought when Ben told her about House Rabbit, what she thought when she saw House Rabbit, why she changed her mind, etc.

Predicting

Use what you know about Melissa to help you work out what she would think.

Think and write

1. What does Ben think House Rabbit has done to his family, and what is his evidence for this?
2. What is the problem with what House Rabbit has done, according to Ben?
3. Why does Ben decide to talk to Melissa?
4. Why do you think Ben decides to sneak round the back and surprise House Rabbit?
5. Where does Ben find House Rabbit?
6. What happens to Ben when he and Melissa go into the kitchen, and why?
7. Why is Ben so cross when he sees what House Rabbit has done in his bedroom?
8. What do you think happens when House Rabbit stares at Ben with 'those raspberry ice-pop eyes'?
9. Why do you think Melissa drags Ben into the garden?
10. Do you think the author makes the character of House Rabbit seem scary or funny? Explain your answer.

Grace the Pirate

Predicting

Read the first paragraph. What clues does it give you about the type of story this is?

Ah, she was a one, that Grace! Who else would have the courage and sense to stay alive on a desert island? Years later, she told me about it. This is her story, if I remember rightly.

She was almost done for when she crawled up the beach, half drowned, scared and very angry. She lay there for a couple of hours. But it was never her way to stay down for long. She staggered to her feet and started to explore.

Straight away she saw that there were banana, coconut and date palms. Now, at least, she had food.

Shaking off her tiredness, she shinned up a coconut palm, and shook down some nuts.

She then broke off several broad green leaves, each bigger than herself. Soon she had also piled up dates and yellow-green bananas.

'At least I won't starve to death,' she told herself.

But besides food she needed somewhere safe to sleep. She picked a spot on the beach, in the open; there she could keep an eye out for passing ships. First she combed the beach for wood. Soon she made a big pile of broken branches, seaweed and grasses – there was even an old sun-bleached oar.

The dried seaweed and grasses covered her floor. She used wood for the walls, slanted like a tent. Then she tied banana leaves over the cracks with coconut fibre.

‘It may not be a palace,’ she sighed, ‘but it’ll do. At least it’ll save me from the worst of the rain, wind and sun.’

The sun was hanging low over the sea. She was stiff and sore – and very hungry. First she ate some dates and bananas, and then she split open a coconut on a stone to drink the sweet milk.

At last, she lay down upon the grass floor in her new house and watched sea-fleas jumping up and down on her new mattress.

‘I’ve got through one day,’ she told herself. ‘Tomorrow, I’ll explore the whole island. Who knows? Maybe I’ll find some company.’

Little did she know she already had some!

Someone was watching her even as she fell asleep.

She must have slept for many hours, for when she awoke, the sun was already high in the sky. What was that noise outside?

Suddenly, she heard it again. Someone was moving about outside the hut. They were creeping up on her – no doubt to slit her throat!

Grabbing her only sandal, she sat up, her heart in her mouth.

All at once, an ugly bearded figure poked its head through the doorway…

She didn’t scream. Instead, she giggled with relief and the bearded figure scuttled away, tail between its legs.

‘A fine pirate you’d make, Billy Goat,’ she cried. ‘Fancy running away at the sight of a girl!’

Then she thought to herself, ‘If I’m kind, you’ll come back. And where there’s a billy, there might be a nanny – and that means milk.’

She sat down on the warm sand and cupped her chin in her hands, gazing out to sea.

‘If only I could catch some fish,’ she thought. ‘But I need a fire to cook them on.’

All of a sudden she had an idea. 'What if I gather some dry leaves and wood bark? I can use this bit of broken glass to focus the sun's rays on the leaves.'

It was worth a try. After collecting some leaves and placing the broken glass between the midday sun and the dry leaves, she sat patiently waiting. Several minutes later, blue-grey smoke began to drift upwards.

This was followed by a sudden burst of flame. Quickly adding more twigs, she soon had a good fire blazing on the sand.

'Now all I need is a fishing line,' she thought. 'I know... What if I twist my earrings into fish hooks? Then I can tie them to string twisted from palm fibre. And I'll stick a bit of crab on the hook as bait. There's my fishing line!'

An hour or so later she was standing on a rock above the sea. Her fishing line was dangling into clear blue water where no one had ever fished before. And in next to no time she had a pile of flapping, shining fish at her feet.

She tossed the tiddlers back, took half a dozen big fish and pushed a stick through each one. Then she strung them across her barbecue.

A delicious smell of grilled fish floated across the sand and into the trees. While she was busy eating, out of the corner of her eye she noticed something moving. There were two shadowy figures among the palm trees.

'Aha,' she said to herself. 'Welcome to dinner, Bill and Nan. If you want food, come and get it.'

She cut up a few bits of date and coconut and left them on the sand next to her.

Slowly but surely, the goats came to eat out of her hand.

Grace the Pirate

Partner activities

I can ...

- read a story and take part in a role-play about what might happen next
- write a playscript based on the role-play

1. Read the story, and then talk about what might happen next for Grace. What if another person came to the island? Who might it be? What might happen? Use your ideas in a role-play where one person plays Grace and the other plays the new person on the island.
2. With your partner, write a short playscript based on ideas from your role-play.

Imagining

Use all your senses to help you imagine what your character would think, feel, see, hear, touch and even taste, as well as what they would do.

Think and write

1. Who do you think is telling this story?
2. How does Grace feel when she reaches the desert island? Explain why she might feel like this.
3. Which things on the desert island help Grace to survive? Name at least three things.
4. Why does Grace build her shelter on the beach?
5. Who is watching Grace as she falls asleep?
6. What does Grace use to help her catch fish?
7. Why does Grace want the billy goat and nanny goat to come to her?
8. Why do the goats come to her?
9. Write three sentences to describe the character of Grace as she is shown in this text.
10. Does the author make you feel sorry for Grace in this text? Explain why, or why not.

Imagining

What type of text do you think this is, looking at the headings, illustrations and types of information included?

APOLLO 13

"Successful Failure"

The story of the Apollo 13 has been told in an exciting Hollywood film starring Tom Hanks as mission commander Jim Lovell. But the real life events that took place during six days in April 1970 gripped people around the world more than any action movie. Officially classified as a "successful failure" Apollo 13 was a mission to the Moon that came within a hair's breadth of disaster. Remarkably, for such a complex project, the simple changes of state, melting, boiling and evaporation, played an important role in the unfolding drama.

On 21 July 1969, Neil Armstrong, commander of Apollo 11, became the first human being to set foot on the Moon. Apollo 11 and its follow-up mission Apollo 12, both landed astronauts on the Moon, then returned them safely to Earth.

By the time Apollo 13 was launched on 11 April 1970 the public were beginning to take the success of Moon missions for granted. But, at 9:08 pm on 13 April, some 200,000 miles from Earth, the crew felt a sharp bang followed by a series of vibrations. Lunar module pilot Jack

Apollo 13: its launch and ground crew in Houston

Swigert saw a warning light flash on and calmly reported over the radio link to Earth, "Houston, we've had a problem here".

Looking out of the window of the command module Jim Lovell saw debris and gas evaporating into space. The instruments showed that one of the mai oxygen tanks was empty and the second was losing pressure rapidly. An explosio had destroyed one tank and badly damaged the other.

The situation was critical – but not yet fatal. The Moon landing was immediate abandoned as the astronauts and grounc crew worked frantically to devise a plan return the crippled craft to Earth.

he craft had not been designed with ıough power to reverse direction in mid-ght, so it had to continue on its outward urney, swinging around the Moon before eading back to Earth. In the meantime e crew moved into the lunar-landing odule to use the oxygen, water and ower supplies that it carried.

he crew spent the following days in eezing temperatures with just a cupful of ater to drink each day as they conserved eir remaining power and water supplies. ıt the plan went well. A few hours before nding they returned to the dark ommand module, switched on its electric rcuits, and prayed that there would be ıough power left for a safe touchdown. ith baited breath the ground crew aited. Then, at 12:07 pm on 17 April, early four days after the explosion that reatened to maroon them in space, eering erupted as the crew of Apollo 13 ırachuted safely into the Pacific Ocean.

onths later the official report ı the mission showed that the llowing sequence of events ıd led to the explosion.

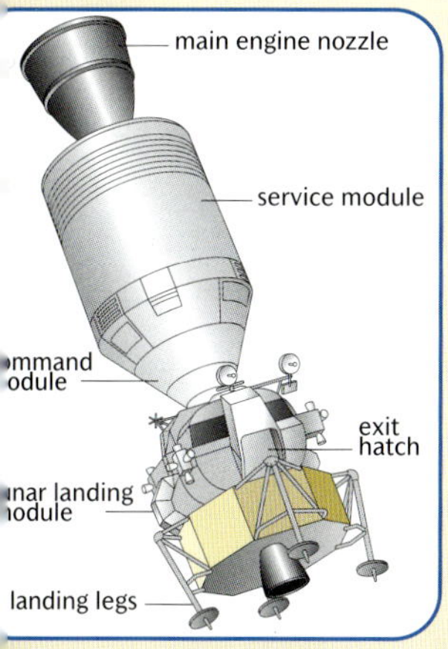

Apollo 13 at the time of the explosion

Apollo 13 astronauts

Day before launch

- The liquid oxygen tank was not working properly.
- Engineers used an electric heater inside the tank to boil off liquid oxygen.
- The insulation on a faulty switch melted.
- The problem was not noticed.

Two days after launch

- The astronauts were told to turn on the fan inside the tank to stir the liquid oxygen.
- The faulty insulation caught fire.
- The tank exploded.
- Oxygen from the tank evaporated into space.

In terms of its goal to land men on the Moon, Apollo 13 was a failure. But because the astronauts and ground crew were able to use their knowledge and skills to overcome disaster without loss of life, it can be safely described as a "successful failure".

Apollo 13

Partner activities

I can ...

- **read and compare two texts**
- **point out some of the differences and similarities between the two texts**

1. Read the text, and briefly discuss with your partner what it is about.
2. Now turn to page 24 in this book, and read the text on that page. With your partner, make a list of the main differences and similarities between the two texts. Think about the way the texts are written, as well as the information they contain. Which text do you prefer, and why?

Summarising

Think about what each text is *mostly* about. What is the author trying to tell us in each text?

Think and write

1. When was Apollo 13 launched?
2. What happened to the oxygen tanks on Apollo 13 on 13 April?
3. Why did the crew move into the lunar landing module?
4. What were conditions like in the lunar landing module?
5. Were the astronauts and ground crew confident that they could get Apollo 13 safely back to Earth? Find a quotation to show this.
6. Why did the astronauts need to conserve power?
7. What was the original cause of the problem with Apollo 13's oxygen tanks?
8. How many people died on the Apollo 13 mission?
9. Explain why the Apollo 13 mission was called a 'successful failure'. Was that a good description? Why, or why not?
10. This text comes from a book called *Changing State*. Why do you think it was included in that book?

Petey (1)

Questioning & clarifying

As you read, think about differences and similarities between Sophie's life and your life.

Sophie Mum! Dad! I'm home!

Mum Swing round! Blast them with your laser!

Dad You scurvy dog! I'll make you walk the plank!

__Sophie__ narrates.

Sophie There they are, as usual, with their helmets on, and both plugged into it. The machine plays a film in the helmet, and it's as if you're in it. It seems like the real world, but it isn't. Me and my brother Sam aren't allowed to go on it, but Mum and Dad are on it all the time. Mum's favourite is the Space Wars programme.

Mum Got them! Set controls to Warp Speed Factor 9 and let's get out of here!

Sophie And Dad's is the Pirate programme.

Dad Yo ho ho, mateys! Set a course for the Spanish Main!

__Sophie__ narrates.

Sophie I look at them and think how stupid they look, talking to themselves with those daft helmets on. Then I decide I'd be better off going into the kitchen and talking to Petey instead.

We move to the kitchen, where __Petey__ the robot is busy preparing food in the Food Dispenser.

When __Petey__ speaks, his voice is flat and robotic.

Petey Good afternoon. Please wait while I scan my data banks for your name. Ah. There it is. Hello, Sophie.

Sophie Hello, Petey. What are you up to?

Petey I am preparing your meal in the Food Dispenser, Sophie. It will be ready for you soon.

__Sophie__ narrates.

Sophie Petey's our domestic robot – a model PT-3000. That's how he got his name – Petey. He's really old-fashioned and his memory-circuits are slow. Dad was going to get a new one, but then he went and bought that stupid Ultra-Reality Machine instead. I'm glad, though. I like Petey. He's been around for as long as I can remember.

We go back to the kitchen.

Petey Terrible weather we're having, aren't we... Sophie?

Sophie No, Petey, we're not. We're in the middle of a heat-wave.

Petey Are we? I'm so glad. If you will excuse me, I must return to my work now.

Sophie Of course.

__Petey__ goes back to work, and we hear the Food Dispenser grinding and whirring. Then there is the sound of a buzzer, and the __house computer__ speaks.

Computer Good afternoon. I am pleased to announce that you have a visitor.

Sophie A visitor? Who is it?

Computer He says his name is Sam.

Sophie Sam? That's not a visitor! That's my brother!

Computer Oh. Of course. I do apologize for my error. I shall let Sam in straight away.

__Sophie__ speaks to __Petey__.

Sophie There's something definitely wrong with our house computer, Petey. That's the second mistake it's made.

Petey (1)

Partner activities

I can ...

- **think of some good and bad points about the situation described in a text**
- **take part in a role-play to explore this**

1. Read the text, and then talk about what life is like for Sophie. Does her life sound fun, or not? Think about her family life, the technology she has in her house, etc.
2. With your partner, role-play being Sophie and her best friend. The best friend should ask Sophie how she feels about her home and family, what she likes, what she would change, etc. Perform your role-play for another pair or for your teacher.

Summarising

Read the text carefully and make some notes to help you sum up the good and bad things in Sophie's life.

Think and write

1. What are Mum and Dad doing when Sophie gets home?
2. Think of three words to describe Mum and Dad and explain why you chose them.
3. Who is Dad talking to when he says 'You scurvy dog!'?
4. Why does Sophie decide to go and talk to Petey?
5. Why do you think Sophie is so fond of Petey?
6. Do you think Petey is fond of Sophie?
7. What is Petey doing when we first meet him?
8. What does Sophie think of the Ultra-Reality Machine? Find two quotations that show this.
9. Why do you think she feels like this about the Ultra-Reality Machine?
10. This play has been written as a radio play. Read the stage directions, and explain how they would help you if you were putting on a radio play.

Questioning & clarifying

How many different types of information can you find in this text?

Roman Letters

When the Romans came to Britain common soldiers wrote to distant relatives and friends describing their lives, ordering food, complaining about mistreatment, and even sending birthday invitations.

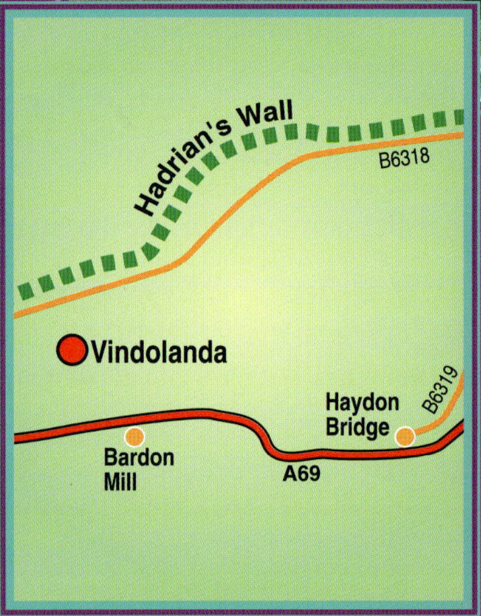

Many of these letters, written in the first and second centuries, have been found at the fort of Vindolanda, just south of Hadrian's Wall, near the border of Scotland and England. They were written in ink on postcard-sized sheets of wood. One from Claudia Severa, the wife of the **garrison** commander Aelius Brocchus, asks a sister to come for her birthday. It is one of the earliest letters written by a Roman woman that has been found.

Claudia Severa to her Lepidina greetings. On 11 September, sister, for the day of the celebration of my birthday, I give you a warm invitation to make sure that you come to us, to make the day more enjoyable for me by your arrival, if you are present. Give my greetings to your Cerialis. My Aelius and my little son send him their greetings. I shall expect you, sister. Farewell, sister, my dearest soul, as I hope to prosper, and hail.'

Nowadays you don't have to write on a piece of wood to send a birthday invitation. You can buy one already printed, and all you have to do is fill in the details. But if you want to write your own, like Claudia Severa, remember to:

- say how you are planning to celebrate your birthday, for example, if you are going swimming, or wearing fancy dress
- put the place, date and time of the party
- send it in plenty of time before the party
- make sure your friends tell you whether they are coming by putting the letters RSVP at the bottom of the invitation. They stand for 'Répondez s'il vous plaît', which is French for 'please reply'.

You are invited to come to my birthday party

at 4 Churchill Drive

on 14 July

starting at 2.00pm

Bring your swimming costume and a towel!

R.S.V.P. 7 July

Roman Letters

Partner activities

I can ...

- work out the key features of a piece of text
- write a new text in the same style

1. With your partner, read the letter from Claudia Severa and make notes on how this is different from a modern letter. Look in particular at the way the letter starts and finishes.
2. Together, write a reply from Claudia Severa's sister saying that she would like to come to the birthday party. Try to make your letter sound like Claudia Severa's letter.

Summarising

When you are summing up the differences between Claudia Severa's letter and a modern letter, it may help to try 'translating' Claudia Severa's letter into more modern language.

Think and write

1. Name two of the reasons why Roman soldiers wrote letters, according to the text.
2. What do you think the photograph on page 50 shows, and why did the author include it?
3. What did Roman soldiers write their letters on?
4. What job did Aelius Brocchus do, and where was he based?
5. What is important about the letter from Claudia Severa to her sister?
6. What was the name of Claudia Severa's sister?
7. Who do you think Cerialis was?
8. When was Claudia Severa's birthday?
9. Why do people put RSVP at the bottom of a letter, and what do the initials stand for?
10. How many different types of text can you find on page 51, and what are they?

Climbing in the Dark

Imagining

As you read, think about how each of the characters is feeling and why. How would you have felt if you were them?

'He's gone!' Mr Fry shouted at me. 'The skinny rat's gone!'

Mrs Hutton, red in the face and holding her skirts in both hands, was running up the main staircase.

'Mr Fry!' she said. 'Whatever is all this racket?'

'That ratbag of a boy's gone up the chimney but he ain't come down.'

'Oh, my stars. The poor mite!'

'Poor? I'll have his bones for broth when I get hold of him.'

Mrs Hutton took a deep breath and clapped her hands, as if that would be enough to calm him down.

'Don't clap at me, missus. I ain't a bird.'

'Then stop flapping. He hasn't done it on purpose, has he?'

He scowled and was about to answer back when there was another shout, a high-pitched scream which came from the other end of the corridor.

'Lawks!' said Mrs Hutton. 'It's Miss Harriet. Come along, Tess. We must see what's up.'

She bustled down the corridor, leaving me to follow.

'What about the missing rat?' Mr Fry called after her.

'He's just taking a rest, poor thing. He'll turn up.'

'But …'

'Don't make a fuss, Mr Fry,' said Mrs Hutton, turning so sharply to shout at him that I almost bumped into her. 'You know where he went. Why don't you stick your head up the chimney and look for him!'

And she hurried away before he could answer. She wheeled round a corner, tilting like a cart stacked with hay. By this time the shouting was much fainter, as if Harriet had run out of breath.

We came to her door and Mrs Hutton flung it open.

I saw a pretty room with lace curtains at the window, two little padded chairs, and a huge, shiny rocking-horse in the middle of the floor. There was no sign of Miss Harriet but we heard her trembling voice.

'Help me, Mary. Please.'

She was crouched in a corner, her hands over her ears.

'There, there, Miss Harriet,' said Mrs Hutton. 'You're quite safe ...'

'There's a creature in here. A monster ...'

She pointed with a shaking finger and we saw a black heap on the floor behind the rocking-horse. I knew at once what it was, but I couldn't understand how it came to be there.

'I think it's Will,' I said.

'Oo-er, so it is,' said Mrs Hutton.

'Please, get rid of it,' said Harriet. 'It's left paw prints on the rugs and ...' – she gulped for air and screamed again – 'it's moving!'

Mrs Hutton ran to Harriet and folded her in her arms.

'He won't harm you, miss. It's only Will.'

'Will?'

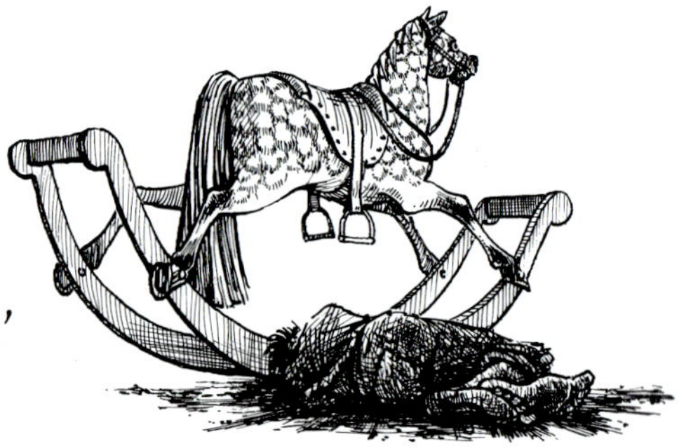

'The chimney sweep's boy. He must've fallen down the chimney and knocked himself out.'

'I don't care what it is, Mary. Just get rid of it.'

'He's not an it; he's a boy.'

Will sat up and rubbed his head. He was so covered in soot that he looked like a big black bird, and there were powdery splashes on the floor around him.

'Where am I?' he moaned. 'What's going on?'

'You're in the nursery, boy,' Mrs Hutton told him. 'You've come down the wrong chimney.'

He blinked and two white eyes appeared in his face. Harriet broke free of Mrs Hutton and dashed to a cord hanging by the door.

She's going to pull the bell, I thought. She's going to call the whole house in here and get poor Will taken away.

Mrs Hutton caught her by the wrist.

'Now you just calm yourself, miss,' she said. 'The little lad's hurt himself and we can't go giving him back to old Fry just yet ...'

'But why not?'

'Because he'll beat him, that's why not,' said Mrs Hutton crossly.

I was amazed that she spoke to her like that. But Harriet did as she was told. She calmed down and pressed herself against the wall, as far from Will as she could get. Mrs Hutton went over to the boy and knelt beside him. She sat him up, gently stroking his face and hair.

'Can't you see?' she said to Harriet. 'He's had a fright.'

Will was shaking, and he'd started to cough again. Mrs Hutton rubbed his back and spoke to him in a soft, kindly voice. Harriet edged away from the wall and came to stand behind Mrs Hutton. She could see now that there was no monster in her room, only a poor frightened boy.

Climbing in the Dark

Partner activities

I can ...

- **work out the author's point of view**
- **work out whether I agree with the author's point of view, and why**

1. Read the text. What do you think the author's point of view is about children being made to work like Will? Discuss this with your partner and decide what you think the author is trying to tell us about working children.
2. Do you agree with the author's view? Explain to your partner why, or why not.

Summarising

Look carefully for clues about the author's point of view – think about what the other characters say and do, and how the author makes us feel sympathy for Will.

Think and write

1. Who is Mr Fry?
2. Why is Mr Fry so angry at the start of the text?
3. Who do you think is the narrator of this story?
4. What does Mrs Hutton think of Mr Fry? Find a quotation that shows this.
5. Why do you think Mrs Hutton feels this way about Mr Fry?
6. What happens to make Harriet scream?
7. How do Harriet's feelings about Will change between the start and the end of the text, and why?
8. Why does Mrs Hutton stop Miss Harriet from ringing the bell?
9. Find one quotation from the text that helps the reader to feel sorry for Will, and explain why you chose this quotation.
10. What kind of person is Mrs Hutton? Write three sentences to describe her.

Petey (2)

Predicting

As you read, think about what might happen next in the story and why.

Petey is a house robot who works in Sophie and Sam's house.

Sam Look, Sophie! He's smiling! Just like he was earlier. Petey's smiling!

Sophie But that's not possible... is it?

Petey A – A – A – A – CHOO!

Sam Petey! What's that noise you're making?

Petey It's supposed to be a sneeze.

Sam A sneeze?

Petey I'm trying to sneeze.

Sam What? Trying to sneeze? Why?

Petey Because I want to. I want to sneeze and I want to – (***Petey** suddenly makes a big burping noise*) Blaaaarrp! – I want to burp, like that. And cough, and sniff, and yawn and feel goose-bumps on my arms and –

Sophie Okay, Petey, we get the picture. But why do you want to do all those things?

Petey Because I want to be more... human.

Sophie More human? But you can't be human. You're a robot.

Petey I know –

Sophie You were made in a factory. You were delivered to our house in a box –

Petey Yes, I know that –

Sophie So how can you be human?

Petey (*Burping*) Blaaarrrpp! There! Did it again! A burp!

Sam No, that's not quite right, Petey.

	If you want to burp, it has to sound more like this –
Sophie	All right, Sam! There's no need for you to join in.
Sam	But I only want to help –
Sophie	I think we can leave the burps out of this.
Sam	I'll show you how later, Petey.

Petey	Thank you, Sam. That's very kind of you.
Sophie	Listen, Petey. Just being able to sneeze and cough... and things like that... it won't make you more human, you know.
Petey	Oh, yes. I understand that. It's only the start. There are other ways. Such as the writing of poetry.
Sam	Poetry?
Petey	(*Proudly*) I have begun to write poetry.
Sam	Write poetry?
Petey	Yes. If you would both be kind enough to listen, here is my first poem.

__Petey__ gives a machine-like cough, then speaks.

There was a young robot named Neil
That liked to eat things made of steel
Dessert was tin foil
Which he washed down with oil
Then he said, 'What a fabulous meal!'

Well? What do you think?

Petey (2)

Partner activities

I can ...

- compare the way a character is portrayed in two texts
- take part in a role-play to explore the character

1. Read the text, and then read the other extract from *Petey*, on pages 47-48 of this book. What differences do you notice between Petey in the earlier extract and Petey in this extract? With your partner, discuss why Petey might have changed.
2. One of you should role-play Petey, and the other should role-play either Sam or Sophie. In your roles, have a conversation about how and why Petey has changed, and what might happen next.

Imagining

Imagine you were Petey. How might you feel? What would you want to happen next, and why?

Think and write

1. Why do you think Sam and Sophie are surprised that Petey is smiling at the start of the text?
2. Why do you think Petey is smiling?
3. Why does Petey want to sneeze and burp?
4. How does Sophie feel about Petey trying to burp? Find a quotation that shows this.
5. Which of the three characters do you think is the most important in this scene? Explain why.
6. How does Petey feel about being able to sneeze, burp and write poetry? Find a quotation that shows this.
7. Why do you think Petey thinks writing poetry might make him more human?
8. What do you think Sophie and Sam will say about Petey's poem, and why?
9. Why does Sophie think that Petey can't be human?
10. Do you think that Sophie is right that Petey can't be human? Why, or why not?

From *The Power of Nature* by Becca Heddle, TreeTops Non-Fiction Stage 14, pages 6–7

Summarising

What do you think is the main message of this text?

All about the Sun

- Did you know that the Sun is a star? It looks much brighter than all the other stars because it is very much closer to us. It is 150 million kilometres away – and the Earth would fit inside it more than a million times.
- Here's a way to get an idea of this scale.

You will need:

- a peppercorn (to represent the Earth)
- a football (to represent the Sun)
- a football field
- a friend

Ask your friend to hold a peppercorn at one end of the football field.

Take the football and run down the pitch, stopping about a quarter of the way down the field (about 26 metres).

If the Earth was the size of a peppercorn, this is how far it would be from the Sun.

- But what is a star? A star is a ball of very hot gas. It shines because it is making massive amounts of energy deep inside.
- This energy process uses vast amounts of raw materials. Every second the Sun loses about 4 million tonnes of mass which it cannot replace. But it has been working at this rate for nearly 5 billion years, and can last several billion more.
- The Sun makes a terrifying amount of heat. Its surface temperature is estimated at about 5700 degrees Celsius – remember, water boils at 100 degrees Celsius. The Sun's centre is even hotter: about 15 million degrees Celsius. No wonder the Sun's heat can burn your skin, even though that heat has travelled millions of kilometres to reach you.

This is the size relationship between the Earth (the peppercorn) and the Sun (the football).

All About the Sun

Partner activities

I can ...

- carry out an experiment mentioned in the text
- comment on how effective the experiment was

1. Read the text, and find the part of the text that describes an experiment.
2. With your partner, carry out the experiment. (You can use a very small piece of gravel if you can't find a peppercorn.)
3. How effective was the experiment in helping you to get an idea of the size difference and distance between the Earth and the Sun? Write some notes on what you learned from doing the experiment and how effective it was.

Imagining

How well does the experiment help you to picture the size difference and distance between the Sun and the Earth?

Think and write

1. How far away is the Earth from the Sun?
2. Why does the Sun look brighter than the other stars?
3. What are stars made of?
4. Is the Sun getting heavier or getting lighter as time goes on? Explain why.
5. Do you think these changes in the Sun are worrying from the point of view of people living on Earth? Explain why or why not.
6. Which is the hottest part of the Sun, and how hot is it?
7. The heat from the Sun has to travel millions of kilometres to reach Earth – why is it that the Sun's heat is still strong enough to burn our skins?
8. Why do you think the author chose to include the picture of a football in this text?
9. How many different text types can you find in this text, and what are they?
10. Which piece of information about the Sun in this text do you think is most interesting? Explain why.

'The Way Through the Woods' by Rudyard Kipling from Oxford Literacy Web, *The Way Through the Woods and other poems*, pages 48–49.

Summarising

What story is this poem telling?

The Way Through the Woods

They shut the road through the woods
    Seventy years ago.
Weather and rain have undone it again,
    And now you would never know
There was once a road through the woods
    Before they planted the trees.

It is underneath the coppice and heath,
    And the thin anemones.
    Only the keeper sees
That, where the ring-dove broods,
    And the badgers roll at ease,
There was once a road through the woods.

Yet, if you enter the woods
Of a summer evening late,
When the night-air cools on the trout-ringed pools
Where the otter whistles his mate,
(They fear not men in the woods,
Because they see so few)
You will hear the beat of a horse's feet
And the swish of a skirt in the dew,
Steadily cantering through
The misty solitudes,
As though they perfectly knew
The old lost road through the woods...
But there is no road through the woods.

Rudyard Kipling

The Way Through the Woods

Partner activities

I can ...

- understand the meaning of a poem
- work with my partner to create a dramatic reading of the poem

1. Read the poem, and talk with your partner about what it means. What atmosphere is the poet trying to create?
2. Practise reading the poem out loud with your partner. Try to read it in a way that will help listeners understand the story and enjoy the atmosphere. Use sound effects and musical instruments if you like. When you are happy with your reading, you could record it on to tape or perform it for your teacher or another pair.

Imagining

Think about what you might see, hear, feel, smell and even taste if you were there in the wood.

Think and write

1. How long has the road through the wood been closed?
2. What do you think the poet means by 'Weather and rain have undone it again'?
3. What is growing on top of the road now?
4. What is it that only the keeper can see?
5. Which animals and birds live in the woods?
6. What might you see and hear if you went into the woods late one summer evening?
7. Do people often go into the woods? Find a quotation that helps to show this.
8. 'You will hear the beat of a horse's feet/And the swish of a skirt in the dew'. Why might you hear those things? What is unusual about them?
9. Write one or two sentences to describe the atmosphere in this poem.
10. Think of a new effective title for the poem and explain why you chose it.